Why Are You Crying, Daddy?

Why Are You Crying, Daddy?

Kenny Sanford

Courier Publishing
Greenville, SC

Courier Publishing
100 Manly Street
Greenville, South Carolina 29601
CourierPublishing.com

Why Are You Crying, Daddy?

ISBN 978-1-940645-94-0

Printed in the United States of America

Dedication

To my wife, Jane: Your faith and strength were what I admired during very difficult days.

To all of our family: Your unwavering love was truly a gift from God.

Contents

Introduction

Is all life precious? Or is it only when everything is "normal"? You've heard it said, "All we want is for our baby to have ten toes and ten fingers." But what is normal? What happens when there aren't ten toes and ten fingers?

I believe it is God who gives value to life when He breathes into us life itself. It is one reason I wanted to write this book. Many try to determine value of life by a set of standards that men have developed, instead of using God's standards. Of course, every parent wants the best for their children. And I don't think there is anything wrong with that. We all want the best for our kids.

But the individuality of each person makes them unique and loved by God. In our family, what some would count as a tragedy, we've been able to see as a blessing. We certainly don't have all the answers, and we know there are many situations more challenging than ours. All we can speak to is what we have experienced.

In these pages, I am attempting to demonstrate the value of all life — even life that some would not count as valuable.

Life is really a variety of stories, some of which have much meaning and can teach us lessons. That is what I've tried to include: memories that meant something special to me. It is my hope that they will also mean something to you.

Many things have been very painful to write about, but I offer this as a personal testimony to how God has blessed and sustained our family and gives value to all life.

My hope and prayer is that by reading this book you will better understand the value of life. And my prayer is also that if you do not have a relationship with God, you will better understand how much He loves you.

We're Having a Baby!

"Why are you crying, Daddy?" In light of the events of the prior six weeks, it was one of the strangest questions I'd ever heard.

Almost twenty-eight years earlier, a similar day had begun, when we were blessed with a special son. However, on that day, we were in disbelief, and we certainly did not feel very blessed. We had no idea at that time that God had opened up heaven and poured His blessings on our family.

Where do I begin to tell the story of someone who not only was part of us, but became our best friend and helped shape our lives and family?

A heartbreaking miscarriage had ended our first pregnancy. We had often prayed together that God would give us a child, and to lose our first child had been devastating to us.

A year later, my wife, Jane, was pregnant again.

As it is with most couples, we were so excited that we would finally have the child we had prayed to receive. We were often asked, "Do you want a boy or a girl?" I had always loved little girls, but it really didn't matter.

Jane read of a "Drano test," in which one could determine the sex of the baby before an ultrasound was able to. It was done by using Drano and a specimen from that morning. By observing the color, one could supposedly determine whether the baby was going to be a boy or a girl. We still have a photo showing that our test predicted a boy. Of course, any test has a fifty percent chance of being correct!

As the days went on, my wife worried because she didn't feel much movement. However, my mom said I didn't move much either, so we wrote it off as "like father, like son." But my wife's worry grew until she finally persuaded the doctor to do an ultrasound. (During the early 1980s, ultrasounds were not performed as routinely as they are now.)

We were not prepared for what the test showed. The technician very matter-of-factly told us that our son was showing fluid on the brain, a condition known as hydrocephalus. Our doctor explained that the fluid building up on our child's brain could cause damage. He recommended that we go immediately to a specialist at a larger hospital in Columbia, South Carolina. There, the specialist confirmed the diagnosis. It was urgent that our baby be delivered as soon as possible, even though the due date was still a month away.

A lung test was ordered to ensure that our baby could survive an early delivery, and the birth was scheduled for the next day. It seemed that we were at least doing something to help our child have the best possible chance for a good outcome. Even though the diagnosis was not what most parents would hope for, it seemed the doctors were confident and felt that our son would be well cared for.

The shock of having a son born with health problems was having an effect on me. I realized I did not have the strong faith that I had thought I had. Even as I write these words many years later, it is difficult to reflect on those days.

My mind went back to another special boy who

had been born years before, my brother Kevin. Kevin suffered brain damage at birth, so I knew just a little about the difficulties of dealing with a child with special needs. Please allow me to give a little background on our family in the following chapter.

Our Family's Treasure

During the years when I was growing up, we were a typical family in our community. Looking back, I know my parents struggled to provide for me and my older brother, as did most parents, in our community. Of course, we never went hungry and never considered ourselves underprivileged. Clothes handed down from friends were gladly accepted by my parents. I never remember them complaining about money. They were an example to us on how earthly things do not buy happiness.

There was love between my parents, Bunnie and Howard Sanford, that money could not buy. As it was with most people of their time, they both came up amid hard times and learned to be happy despite their circumstances. Neither had electricity or indoor plumbing during their childhoods. Both worked on family farms and knew the struggle it took just to survive. My mom grew up in a wooden farmhouse just a few miles from the house I would later grow up in, and we visited my mom's old home often when I was growing up.

Mom had thirteen brothers and sisters, and when we had a family reunion there were enough cousins to field both sides of the baseball games! We played right next to that beautiful hand-built wood frame house. Amazingly, there was always a cool breeze on the front porch, no matter how hot it was. Inside was always warm and welcoming. My grandmother and her son, Uncle Albert, lived there. Both were such fine Christian people.

I remember Mom talking about picking cotton with her siblings. When they'd complain about their backs aching, their dad (my granddad, whom I never got to meet) would say, "You don't have a back!" I think most who came through those difficult times in our country's history — the Great Depression and World War II — appreciated things more than people do today.

My older brother Bert and I also learned the value of work early in life. We both grew up working on our Uncle David's family farm, which was my Dad's side of the family, with his three sons. I was only about five when one of his sons let me drive the pickup while sitting on his lap. I'd drive it in the ditch, and then he would get it out and I'd run it in the other side. I don't think my mom ever knew about my early driving lessons.

What an amazing opportunity to grow up working on a farm. Uncle David's sons called me Kokomo, which was a funny chimpanzee on television during that time. It's a name that stuck with them most of my life.

It was a time that neither of us would ever forget, and it would forever shape our lives.

Uncle David always insisted on being fair when he carried his products to the market. I remember that he would make sure that size and quality of produce on the top of his truck was the same all the way through. Buyers would remember his honesty and become repeat customers, seeking him out at the South Carolina State Farmers Market.

After a hot day of working in the fields, it was a treat to be asked to go to the market with him to sell the produce. One of the fringe benefits of going was that it was an "all you can eat" adventure at the local canteen. However, the mosquitoes evidently enjoyed the same fringe benefits, as they would almost eat us alive while we waited, sometimes for several days, to sell the produce.

I can still smell the sweet aroma of freshly plowed earth. There is nothing more beautiful than to see plants beginning to pop through the ground after many hours of hard work preparing and planting and sweating.

I also came to know the many dangers of farming. Once, when I was helping Uncle David unload corn into a tractor-driven auger, his sweater got caught in one of the turning joints. When I looked over the side of the trailer, I saw a sight I'll never forget. The auger had pulled him into the joint and ripped the flesh from under his arm. He calmly told me to go have someone call the hospital and tell them he was on the way. I really thought he was going to die, as the wound looked so severe. Thankfully, he made a full recovery.

On another occasion, I came within inches of being killed when I fell off a tractor while riding on the wheel fender (something that should never be done!). My cousin stopped the tractor just before the disc being pulled behind it ran over me.

Of course, coming in from the fields at lunchtime to home-cooked meals from my Aunt Mattie's kitchen, including fresh biscuits or yeast rolls, made all the work worthwhile!

I remember my first childhood experience with grief. Aunt Mattie and Uncle David lost one of their adult sons. I'm sure they both suffered, but I especially remember Aunt Mattie holding me as she wept, grieving for her sudden loss. The death of her son was overwhelming to her, but at the time it did not really touch me as it would today.

Most people who have not had the privilege of working on a small family farm can't fully appreciate where their food comes from. It's there on the front line, where you can see the hand of God each day, and it takes an incredible amount of faith.

My brother still farms today, and I miss those days very much. But it was during those days of hard work that we both, just like our parents, developed a keen sense of what it took to make it through times of adversity. Tough times would come for our family, as they do for most families.

However, during our childhood, America was entering a time of prosperity. Television and electricity were prevalent, unlike our parents' early days, when their lives were similar to colonial times. I often joke that we had "high-definition" black-and-white television during my childhood and that my family did not have a microwave — all we had was an electric oven!

When I first heard that my mom was going to have a baby, I remember crying hysterically. I don't know why. (I'm sure my Dad cried, also!) My older brother was fourteen, and I was twelve. I had been the "baby" for all of my life. Dad even called me "baby" most of my childhood, until the real babies arrived. I guess I was upset because I wouldn't be the baby anymore. To say this pregnancy was unexpected was an understatement. However, we had no idea how much this would eventually change our lives for the better. But at twelve, you really don't get very philosophical.

My Dad was fifty at the time. In those days, dads did not go in the delivery room. Instead, they waited bravely outside for word to come. Also, I don't remember the word "pregnant" being used back then. The words "expecting" or "in a family way" were more common. The sex was not even known before the birth, as this was before there were ultrasounds. (And I don't remember the word "sex" being used, either!) Mom seemed unusually large. But to a twelve-year-old, I guess any size would have seemed so.

While my Dad waited, a nurse updated him. She told him one baby had been born and they thought there were two more. He told me later that he put his hands out and backed against a wall. As it turned out, there were only two — a boy and a girl! They were named Kay Emily and Kevin David (after my Uncle

David).

I don't remember worrying much about Kevin. I'm sure my parents did, though. It was obvious, looking back, that something was very wrong. I remember his screams at night were almost bloodcurdling. His twin, Kay, thrived and developed as most kids do. I think the doctors just said his stomach had not developed properly. Eventually, my parents started making the rounds of doctors, trying to get to the root of the problem. It was finally determined that Kevin had apparently suffered brain damage at birth, possibly from the umbilical cord wrapping around his neck, cutting off his oxygen.

However, despite Kevin's disability, he was a unique human being whom God had placed in our family. We came to love him so very much — not because of his disability, but because of who he was.

What we've discovered with Kevin is that he's more normal than not. A big mistake many of us make is judging the outside of a person. Of course, it's the first thing our eyes see, so we automatically begin making judgments. But it's when we really get to know the person that we realize the outside is just a wrapper. It's the inside that really matters and what makes all of us who we are.

Kevin not only has feelings, but deep feelings. I remember when he was part of a boys' group at church. One night when games were being played, one of the kids told him he was not included. He might have been mentally challenged, but his feelings were just as normal as anyone's. He started crying, because he just wanted to be included.

On the outside, some people may not seem as "normal" as others. But many of them are more like what I would want to be like than some so-called "normal" people. Their love is genuine, not based on the premise of "What can I get from you?"

'Kevinomics'

If Kevin's view of economics were ever adopted, it would turn the whole monetary system upside down. The world would never be the same. Even gold would be worthless. The president would have to summon world leaders for an emergency summit. To Kevin, one dollar means just as much as a thousand. Money is not something he worries about unless he needs gas (which he calls water) for his golf cart. If someone does something for him, he holds out his hand, signaling HE wants money! If you give him money, five one-dollar bills mean more than a thousand-dollar bill!

Maybe there's a lesson here. Kevin's happiness does not depend on money. He's content even when money is low. He'd much rather have your friendship and take a ride on his golf cart than any number of dollars. I think parents and families can take a lesson from that. Sometimes parents tend to throw presents out to their kids in an attempt to buy happiness. But kids would much rather have the time. Why? Because it is time that is priceless!

Kevin's Theology

How deep is Kevin's understanding of God? He probably would not do real well on a seminary test. But his simple faith is really a lot of what Jesus taught. Whenever someone has sickness or trouble,

Kevin insists that someone pray for that person whenever the blessing is said or if a visit is being made. He also will call someone and "pray" with them over the phone. How do we know that is what he's doing? We just learn what he is saying, and know!

Kevin, of course, does not believe in drinking! If you offer him a soft drink, he refuses and starts staggering like a drunk, imitating how he would be if he were to drink it.

Christmastime

Christmas has always been a special time with our family. Not only is it a celebration of our Lord's birth, but we've always enjoyed all of the festivities of the Christmas season, including family time. Kevin usually has one item that he wants, and he talks about it the entire season. His speech is very limited, and you just have to learn some of what he means — or at least learn the "sign language" he has developed for it.

His best Christmas gift was the golf cart I've already mentioned, which our family surprised him with a few years ago. Nothing will ever top that. He has never gotten over it, and he always invites people to come ride with him. One does not have to be a close friend to receive an invitation. In fact, you don't even have to know him! He'll invite waitresses, or anyone who stops to talk with him just a minute.

One year he began telling my sister-in-law Donna about a "shoe." She kept telling him, "Kevin, your shoes are fine." But he kept insisting about the "shoe." Somehow Donna had missed it, but Jane and I already knew: "Shoe" is how he says "tree." He was asking where her Christmas tree was!

Sign Language

Kevin can say only a few words. Sometimes a word will come out and he gets so excited and laughs, but seldom can he repeat it. Most of his communication is through sign language. I don't mean International Sign Language. It's a whole language he develops as he goes. If he's around people, he's continuously babbling, trying to tell others what's happened in his life.

If he were able to speak clearly, I'm sure he would be known as a "motor mouth."

Some have asked me, "How do you know what he's saying?" Of course, it is a big advantage if you already know the events of the week. He begins doing charades, trying to communicate what's bursting to come out. Sometimes, I sense the frustration. But usually his infectious smile and laughter are what's prevalent.

Snow Man

I guess Kevin developed his love for snow from our mom. I'm not sure where Mom got it. Being from South Carolina, it's not like she grew up in snow country. I still remember Mom staring out the window, grinning and looking for the first of a few flakes to begin falling. She loved it so. Maybe it's because it was such a rare event. She was just like a child at the thought of even a dusting.

Kevin must have gotten it from her. Does it matter if it's seventy degrees outside? No, all he has to see is a story on the Weather Channel about it snowing a thousand miles away, and he starts calling. He says, "Call?" which means he wants us call him when it starts. "Kevin, it's too warm for snow!" But it falls on deaf ears. His joy comes from hoping it will snow and someone will bring a four-wheeler and drive around in it. That is heaven for him!

Working Man

For many years, Kevin was privileged to go to a workshop for mentally disadvantaged folks. Of course, Kevin never looked upon it as a privilege. He made many friends with the clients and supervisors. A van would come to pick him up and the driver would blow the horn. That became Kevin's way of talking about going to work. He called it "bonk, bonk" for the sound the horn makes. When asking if he has to go to work, he says, "Bonk, bonk, no?" "Yes, Kevin you're going tomorrow," — followed by the phone slamming down!

Like many of us, Kevin would much rather be on vacation than at work. If you ever want to get on Kevin's bad side, just mention going to work. If our pastor ever even mentions work in his sermon, Kevin shouts "No!" and then follows up with his infectious smile. I've had to mention it to visiting pastors so that they understood that it was nothing personal.

Kevin learned quickly how to avoid work. He had seen my dad wave the van by on days when Kevin was sick. So Kevin started going out on the porch and waving it by, until Dad finally caught on to what he was doing. Just recently, we decided to let Kevin "retire" from work. I think he'll be able to adapt real well.

A Big Heart

You've probably never been loved like Kevin can love. I think his love is more what real love should be. He does not love you for the money you have or who you know or the position you have. (However, it does help if you own a four-wheeler or golf cart!) His love and hugs are real.

Today, through a family effort led by Donna and Kay, we take care of Kevin — not because we have to, but because he is our family's treasure.

Our Son Is Born

For you formed my inward parts; You wove me in my mother's womb. I will give thanks to You, for I am fearfully and wonderfully made; Wonderful are your works, And my soul knows it very well. My frame was not hidden from You, When I was made in secret, And skillfully wrought in the depths of the earth; Your eyes have seen my unformed substance; And in your book were all written the days that were ordained for me, When as yet there was not one of them. (Psalms 139:13-16)

When our son Todd was born, we were prepared for the hydrocephalus, even though that was a very difficult thing to accept. We were unsure as to how much the pressure build-up in his brain might have affected him mentally. The specialist we had been referred to recommended that Jane have a Cesarean section in order to reduce the risk of further injury to him.

The morning of the delivery, the anesthesiologist was just amazing. As I sat on a stool near Jane in the delivery room near, she talked a mile a minute, trying to keep me occupied from all that was going on. I could tell she had done this before, and I really didn't realize what she was doing at the time, but I was very thankful afterward. After Todd's birth, a team of nurses immediately took him and began working with him. The anesthesiologist told me our son had a little something on his back and they would just stitch it up. There was no alarm in her voice, so I gave little thought to it. I went out to my waiting family and told them what we already knew: we were the proud parents of a son — a child we had prayed and hoped for so often!

When I went back to check on Jane, there was a doctor — a neurosurgeon — discussing the situation with her. Very tersely, he said, "We have your son scheduled for surgery on his back."

"What," I asked? "Is there any damage?"

The doctor said, "We can only close his back, we cannot repair any damage." And with that he was off to surgery.

It turned out that he was a very good doctor, and I'm sure he had our son's best interest in mind, but that was all the explanation we would receive for several days. It was a textbook example of how not to explain to very anxious parents about a special-needs baby. It was as if a ton of bricks had fallen on our heads. We were stunned, and I was literally unable to speak. I went back out to tell my family and could only whisper to them the little that I knew.

In addition to the hydrocephalus, Todd was born with spina bifida, or myelomeningocele. It is not uncommon for a child with spina bifida to also have hydrocephalus. Spina bifida is a birth defect where the spine does not close. The neural tube normally begins closing just four weeks after conception. I had never remembered hearing of this defect. There are varying degrees of this condition, depending on how high up the spine the opening is and depending on the amount of damage. Todd would be paralyzed from his abdomen down.

Later that night, we talked with a well-meaning intern. He told us that sometimes the nerves grow back and there is a decrease in paralysis. However, to my knowledge, this is just not the case. I found myself watching our son's toes and getting excited over every little twitch I saw.

The next day, someone gave us an article, "Joy Turned Upside Down," about a child born with problems. There could not have been a better name for our situation: such joy at finally being parents, but also so much to deal with. The joy did seem upside down.

Todd was placed in the neonatal intensive care unit of Richland Memorial Hospital in Columbia, South Carolina. One of the nurses wrote the following on a piece of tape and placed it on the incubator: "Hi, my name is Todd!" Next to him was a little boy born several months premature. His name was Ty. I had never seen a baby so small. He almost did not look like a baby. Over the next days and weeks, Ty clung to the edge of life. Many times his mom would be crying when he stopped breathing or suffered a collapsed lung.

Todd's relationship with Jane's mom, Evelyn, had a rough beginning. When Todd was just a few days old, his first surgery to relieve the pressure from his brain was scheduled. However, the doctor got a virus, and the surgery had to be rescheduled for the next day. After the surgery, the doctor came to the door and asked for his mom and dad to come and talk. As the door separating the waiting room from the conference room was shutting, he said, "I'm sorry." That's all Evelyn heard, and it almost caused her to have a heart attack right there in the waiting room. The entire sentence was actually, "I'm sorry I was sick yesterday."

When Jane was released from the hospital, she began reading a medical book we had in our home. As she read about Todd's condition, the reality of how serious it was hit her, and she began sobbing.

Over the next couple of months, Todd had six more surgeries in an attempt to prevent the excess fluid from building up on his brain. A shunt was installed to relieve the pressure and ran down a tube to his abdomen.

The good thing about shunts is that they are life-saving. The bad thing is that many things can go wrong. Todd's first shunt was sheared off. The neuro-surgeon told us he'd never seen anything like that happen before. He said many parents might have sued the manufacturer. Although there are times when lawsuits are justified, we never really considered it. Instead, we were thankful that there were manufacturers willing to take chances and produce a product that could give our son a chance for life.

One of Todd's shunts, called a ventriculoatrial shunt, was routed to his heart. It got infected, and a blood clot formed. The shunt was completely removed so that the infection could be controlled. We thought we were going to lose Todd before the last surgery, as so many things kept going wrong. The doctor even considered sticking a needle through the top of his head to manually relieve the pressure building in his brain. However, each time he would check the soft spot on our son's head, the pressure had not built up and it was not necessary to do this dangerous procedure. I remember that the doctor was really amazed and just shook his head in disbelief that the pressure was staying down.

However, Todd was not looking very good. His doctor discussed with us the possibility that our son might not make it, as nothing seemed to be going right. The surgeries and infection were taking a toll. He looked so weak and frail. In a photo we have of him from that time, his appearance reminds us how bad off he really was. We just could not imagine losing him!

On Sundays, I was able to escape for a little while and drive back home to our church for worship. Jane seldom left the hospital. She took on the difficult part of staying all of the time. But it was during those drives that I worshiped and prayed. When I got to church, I could have turned around and gone back, because I had already worshiped at the feet of God. I remember praying to God that if He chose to take our son, maybe Todd's life could be used to touch someone else.

I was reminded of the story in the Bible of how Abraham had been told to sacrifice his son Isaac. "He said, Take now your son, your only son, whom you love, Isaac, and go to the land of Moriah, and offer him there as a burnt offering on one of the mountains of which I will tell you" (Genesis 22:2).

Abraham was willing to do this incredible thing, but, of course, it was only a test. God stopped Abraham before the knife plunged. My faith was nothing compared to this.

After Todd's seventh surgery, our prayers had been heard. Miraculously, Todd began recovering and was soon the precious smiling baby we had dreamed of.

A New Life Begins

And so began a new life for Jane and me. We were very proud parents, but so much had changed so fast. A baby by itself brings changes; but a special needs baby, even more.

Our life became a blur of doctor visits, hospital stays, physical therapy, and just trying to learn what we needed to know. There was so much to try to understand. One neurosurgeon told us, "Your son is very complicated." As most parents learn, no instruction book comes with a new baby; that is even more true with a special-needs child.

Eventually, our life evolved to the point that, before we went anywhere, we had to consider if the place was accessible and if Todd would have a somewhere to rest and a place we could take care of his needs.

But despite the trials, it also became a life of incredible rewards — and love. It was a time when we got a little glimpse of how much God really loved us and was giving value to our lives. God loves us where we are and is not impressed by what we can do. His desire is simply for us to have a relationship with Him.

In the Bible, we learn how much Jesus cared for children. We see this in Matthew 19:13-14: "Then some children were brought to Him so that He might lay His hands on them and pray; and the disciples rebuked them. But Jesus said, Let the children alone, and do not hinder them from coming to Me; for the kingdom of heaven belongs to such as these." Jesus cares for all children — those born healthy, those with special needs, and the unborn.

One thing the hospital did that we thought was outstanding was hold a birthday party every year for all the children who had been in the neonatal intensive care unit the previous year. It was a celebration of life. As part of the celebration, there was a crawling contest. The year we attended, Ty, the small premature baby, was also invited. It was Ty who won the contest! To see a baby who was so small that he almost did not look like a baby win the crawling contest a year later was indeed miraculous. It must help the doctors and nurses to see some fruits from all their efforts. They see quite a bit of heartbreak, but to see the good side has to be an encouragement.

Todd's first orthopedic doctor, Dr. Rick, was an amazing man. You could tell that he had a special love for kids with special needs. There was no pretense when he kissed Todd on the cheek. He was the founder of an orthopedic clinic in Columbia. He believed in giving kids every opportunity to have a good life. He even started a family support group that we attended for many years. We got to know other families and their problems. Dr. Rick would become outraged when he talked of doctors in other specialties seemingly not caring about the children.

One of the first things we learned from him is that kids develop as a result of being able to explore. Most kids are running and crawling around and seemingly getting into everything, but at the same time their little brains are filling up with information.

The doctor prescribed a miniature wheelchair so that Todd, at a very young age, could be mobile. He also prescribed a special brace for his back so that sitting would not further damage his spine. It was just amazing how fast Todd learned to roll his chair. It was a small red chair with a handle that allowed us to push him when needed. For a wheelchair, it was extremely cute. It belied the needs it was really taking care of. Out on the beach, many commented on what a unique and cute stroller we had. Most did not realize it was really a wheelchair.

When Todd was a little older, his doctor prescribed a "Parapodium" to allow him to stand and help build bone strength. It was simply a brace with a stand at the bottom so that he could be upright.

Later, he prescribed a special brace known as reciprocating gait orthosis (RGO) so Todd could even walk with the help of a walker. Even though his first steps were not like most kids', they were just as exciting to us. Dr. Rick explained to us that it was important for his bone strength to be upright as much as possible. Between both of these devices,

Todd was able to be more like other kids and "get into things," also!

Political Interests

When Todd was about three, he could point at pictures of each of the presidential candidates and name them. Some of the candidates during this election cycle were George H.W. Bush, Michael Dukakis, Jesse Jackson and Al Gore. He could identify their pictures much better than probably the majority of adults could at the time.

When folks learned this, including Dr. Rick, they were constantly asking him who he wanted for president. Usually, with great emphasis, he would say, "Jesse Jackson!" Folks would roar with laughter and ask him the same question over and over.

A Special Football

When Todd was just a toddler, we used to play imaginary football on the soft carpeted floor. Todd would throw a handkerchief as a penalty flag and say, "Penalty flag on the play! Fifteen-yard penalty!" And then he'd crawl toward me and we'd "tackle" each other. I guess this was just a prelude to his love of the sport. College football was his favorite, but he loved all sports. Whatever was in season, he usually watched, including golf, basketball and baseball. His love of college football probably came from our love of it — especially the South Carolina Gamecocks.

Todd had a large gray rabbit that he always wanted to enter in our local county fair. It had been a gift to him from one of our friends. One year, it so happened that we had to take the rabbit to the fair on the same day the Gamecocks were playing their rival, the Georgia Bulldogs, on television. We told Jane's mom we would be recording the game and asked her not to tell us anything about the game, as she usually watched, too.

On the way to deliver the rabbit, we stopped by her house for a minute. That's when she told me, "I'm watching, but you're not going to like it." I didn't say anything to Jane, but I was infuriated. Why had she told me that, when she knew we'd be watching it later? As I thought about it, I think I was just so mad because the Gamecocks were evidently getting beat and I was not a very good sport.

When we got home and started watching the game, I could not believe it. The Gamecocks played an outstanding game and beat Georgia in a terrific contest. My mother-in-law had played one of the greatest gags on me that had ever been played — and probably ever will be!

One Christmas, Todd asked Santa for an NCAA football. It was easy to find a football, but one with "NCAA" on it was difficult. Jane and I scoured stores trying to help so that Santa would not disappoint. (This was before the days of Internet shopping.) Surely it would not matter if it didn't have "NCAA" stamped on it, as long as it was a football, right? Of course, the first thing Todd did on Christmas morning was to roll it over to see if "NCAA" was on the ball! Thankfully, Santa had found just the right one!

Lost Dog

When children are in the home, there are always learning opportunities for kids and parents. When

Todd was about five years old, we decided to get him a pet that would be good for him.

We read up on different dogs and learned that Shetland sheepdogs were good with kids, and we decided that was the type he needed. We drove all the way to Beaufort, South Carolina, to get one from a breeder we had seen advertised. Todd named the dog Windsor. Where a five-year-old got that name, we could never find out. But the name seemed to fit him. He had so much energy and was such a delight to our family. He lived inside but spent much time outside to burn off energy.

However, one day he went missing. Despite our calling and looking for him all over the community, it was as if he had dropped off the planet. I drove around, frantically looking for him. I remember Todd asking, "Why doesn't he come home? He knows how much I love him." Weeks went by, and all hope for finding our dog again was lost.

One day, a beagle showed up at our house. Todd was so excited about having a dog again. Clearly the dog was lost, as he had a collar with an ID tag.

"Please, can we keep him?" Todd asked. That's when we reminded him about Windsor. If someone found Windsor, wouldn't we want them to let us know? "Yes," Todd had to admit. "Then we need to call the owners of this dog also, don't we?"

One evening we heard a loud bang on the back door. "It's Windsor!" Jane exclaimed. (It was his signature "knock" when he wanted to come in.) And, yes, it was Windsor! Where he had been all of that time, we'll never know. His fur was matted with more stickers than I thought possible, hitchhiking souvenirs he'd picked up on his way back home. Apparently, Windsor really did know how much Todd loved him!

Money in the Bank

Todd first learned about money when he was little. He was usually with his Grandmother Rutland when she cashed her check at the bank.

He started asking if we could buy this or that item. I told him, "No, we don't have the money."

Finally, one day during this discussion he told

me, "Get the money from the bank." I said, "Money has to be paid back to the bank." He had only observed one-way transactions, so he replied, "Uh, uh. Nanny gets money, and she doesn't pay it back!"

Don't Forget About Me

When Todd was little, my job required me to travel. It was interesting work, and I was able to meet people from all over the world. There was nothing I would have liked better than to bring my wife and son with me, but I just was not able to. I always tried to bring back photos and stories so that Todd could share a little of my travels.

Before one trip, Todd, who was about five, kept telling me, "I'm going with you." I would just smile, because I knew he could not possibly go. Besides, I left sometimes at four a.m. to catch my flight, and he would not even know when I was leaving. As I was getting ready that morning, he evidently had planned to wake up, and he said, "Daddy, don't forget about me back here." It broke my heart, and I probably never came closer to missing my flight than on that day.

A Jeep for Todd

As is true with most kids, Todd loved being outdoors. Sitting in a wheelchair in our rural yard was not really very exciting for a growing little boy. When he was a toddler, we decided to get him a battery-powered Jeep to ride around in the yard.

However, the accelerator was designed like cars, where the foot was needed to power it. One of our friends, who was also my sister-in-law Donna's dad, Mr. T., was an accomplished electrician. He rewired the toy Jeep and added a button on the steering wheel to power it. It worked perfectly, and Todd had so much fun riding around our big yard and enjoying a little independence.

Reminded of Our Blessings

I was having one of those days. You know the kind — feeling sorry for how bad everything was. Taking care of a child with disabilities can be challenging, to say the least. When you start down the road of sorrow, things can really begin to look dark. Oh, how bad we have it, I was thinking.

That day, we were at the doctor's office waiting for an appointment. Sometimes it almost seemed like a second home, as we spent much of our life at doctors' offices and hospitals.

Soon, in came a couple with their child. It was obvious this was a challenging situation for this family. I don't remember all the details. They had a machine with some sort of tubing, so one could easily see their difficulty in just coming to the doctor. Soon the dad said, "We need to suction." They switched the machine on and began suctioning their child so that he would be able to breathe.

No one else knew it, but I bowed my head right there and asked God to forgive me for being so ungrateful. We really did not have difficult times, especially compared to others. We were so blessed with a special son and a very loving family.

Weatherman Todd

I'm not sure how it got started, but Todd loved weather. He especially loved seeing the rare snowfalls that we have in the Midlands of South Carolina.

Maybe that part was genetic, as my mom and Todd's Uncle Kevin thought snow was the most beautiful thing in the world. When Todd was just a couple of years old, we sat him on a cookie tray and slid him in the snow. We would even bring a bowl of snow inside so he could enjoy it without the outside cold to contend with.

He enjoyed monitoring the weather, especially hurricanes. He was about seven when the terrible storm Hurricane Andrew struck south Florida with incredible devastation. It was later graded as the most powerful of hurricanes, a category five. The year was 1992. Todd was watching a news report showing all of the incredible destruction and. Of course, the reporters were talking about the Federal Emergency Management Agency (FEMA) and what they were doing to assist people. Todd, excitedly, called out to me, "Dad, if you think Hurricane Andrew was bad, you ought to come and see what FEMA just did!"

Later we purchased an electronic rain, temperature and wind gauge for his room. Whenever a weather event was happening, he would race back to his room, get the reading, and then race back to tell us his weather report. In a few minutes, another report would be due. He would race back to his room again. He watched the Weather Channel so much that we wondered if it had been a good idea to get a satellite dish for him!

Todd Creek Road

Our county decided to implement the 911 emergency service. With that, all the roads needed an official name. The road we lived on was slated to be named Alabaster. It was not a favorite choice of ours — or most on our road, for that matter.

We have a little creek near our house. One of Todd's favorite things when he was young was to go fishing there. There were very few fish, but if you're a kid, who cares?

When Todd saw minnows in the shallows, he would say, "Look — pimento fish!"

When we had fished and were ready to climb back up the steep hill to our home, I would have to pry the fishing cane from his hands as he cried. It didn't matter if we didn't have even had one bite.

One time, as we were leaving after catching nothing at all, Todd said, "I'm going to tell Mom we caught eight."

Another time, I promised him we'd go fishing, but only if he would let me get a thirty-minute nap. Many times we would lie down on the floor and rest. This time there was not so much rest. Every five minutes I'd hear him calculating the time. "Daddy, twenty-five more minutes before we go. Daddy, twenty minutes more before we go!" My nap that day wasn't very beneficial, but the memory still brings a smile to my face.

Because of our experiences by that little creek, the neighbors agreed to name our road Todd Creek Road.

Life Stories

The iPod

One thing I've learned about dads is that we never really grow up. We still have a little boy in us, and we love new gadgets. It's just that our toys usually cost more than kids' toys.

At one time, the iPod Touch was really popular. I really wanted one, but I didn't think it wise to spend the money. Todd spent quite a bit of time bidding on eBay, trying to buy a used one for me. Of course, when bidding on the good ones, he would inevitably get outbid.

One day when we were talking, Todd said he wished he had $200 so he could just buy an iPod. Thinking he had decided he wanted one for himself, I told him he had the money in his savings account. But I also told him I really didn't think he would use the iPod enough. That's when he said, "I wasn't going to get it for me, I was going to get it for you."

Of course, I would not have wanted him to use his money for such an expensive gift. But the gift had already been given, and it was given from the heart. The old sentiment, "It's not the gift, but the thought that counts," is very true. The iPod my son wanted to buy for me might be broken and worn out by now, but the gift from his heart is still new and fresh and means more to me than a million iPods!

A Governor in the Cow Barn

As I said earlier, Todd always loved politics. In 2000, when Todd was in his teens, we heard that Governor George W. Bush was coming to our little town of Orangeburg to campaign for the presidency. We decided it was a great opportunity to see someone on the national stage. Jane even brought along a pen in the shape of an elephant in the hopes of getting an autograph.

The event was held at the Orangeburg County Fairgrounds in the cattle barn. When we arrived, it was as if almost everyone else in the county was there, also. We were at the back of the barn, maneuvering Todd in his chair, back and forth, trying to help him get a glimpse of Governor Bush. The crowds of people and press members lined up in front of us made it an almost impossible task.

After a while, a man came up and asked if we'd like to meet the governor. Of course, we were delighted. He told us to follow him to the front and the governor would meet with us after he was finished speaking.

We were brought up to the front with some others with disabilities, including, as it turned out, one of Todd's cousins, who was also in a wheelchair.

Governor Bush spoke to each one. It was as if we had known him all our lives. What a warm person he was! I don't know whose policy it was to do what they did that day, but we'll never forget it. In the middle of a heated campaign, there was still time for compassion for the less fortunate.

By the way, we did get an autograph, but not with the elephant pen. An enormous Secret Service agent tapped me on my shoulder and asked me to put it away. He said, "The governor has his own pen."

Coach Holtz

As University of South Carolina Gamecocks fans, we had a rare opportunity to go and hear head coach Lou Holtz speak.

Someone had given us tickets to go to the local Gamecock Club for the speech. However, it had been one of those days for me. When I came home that night, I was tired, and going back to Orangeburg was not high on my list. I knew Todd had his heart set on hearing Coach Holtz. If I had asked Todd if it was okay if we didn't go, he would have said he didn't care about going, so I knew better than to ask. Todd rarely thought of himself and usually thought of us first.

If you've never had the chance to hear Coach Holtz speak, put it on your list. What an inspirational speaker he is, and what a warm person, also! He made a special effort to come over and talk to Todd before he began speaking.

We had a similar opportunity one day at the Gamecocks' practice field. I was watching some players run through their drills, and when I turned back around, Coach Holtz had walked over and was talking with Todd. You can just tell when people want to make others feel good.

After Coach Holtz's talk that night at the Gamecock Club, I told people that Todd drove the van home and I ran along beside it! It was so inspiring. I was ready to run through a wall, no matter how tired I had felt earlier!

A Carolina-Clemson VBS

Every year at our church's Vacation Bible School, a mission project was selected, and the kids raised money for it. Sometimes it would include an incentive — someone might have to kiss a pig, for example — anything to draw attention and get the kids excited about raising money.

Todd almost always wore a Carolina Gamecock shirt and was well known for his rabid support of them. Some of our friends would always kid him about never wearing anything else.

One year he was asked about participating in a

contest with another man who was just as rabid about our state's arch-rival team, the Clemson Tigers. The deal was, whichever one raised the least amount of money would have to wear the other team's shirt to church the following Sunday.

Todd had a lot of Gamecock friends at church. They told him, "Don't worry, Todd, you're not going to have to wear that shirt." The Clemson side lost, but it was so close, and Todd sweated it out. He was never asked to do than particular challenge again, and I'm not sure there's a salesman in the world who could have persuaded him to try it again!

A Special Athlete

Our son never scored a touchdown, never hit a home run, never ran a four-minute mile. But what an athlete he was! He loved athletics for what it was supposed to be — fun.

So what made him such a special athlete, even if he didn't hold any Olympic records? It was his heart. He had the heart of a champion, and that's what makes an athlete special.

When I see athletes throwing away opportunities, I become very upset. What Todd would have done just to be able to walk out on the football field of the Carolina Gamecocks, let alone play for them.

Once, we were able to go out on the field at Williams-Brice Stadium during a fan appreciation day. There were various trophies on display and games for the little kids to play. As I rolled Todd toward the end zone, I imagined him playing there and running toward the goal line. I wondered if he was having the same thoughts.

I know that a lot of the kids with the chance to play college sports are young and make foolish mistakes. Many have not had a background based on godly principles. However, I just want to grab them by their shirt collar and ask, "Don't you understand the opportunity you've been given?"

Todd never complained about not being able to play. While I'm sure he would have loved to have the opportunity, I also think he was content to enjoy the sports. He enjoyed watching and following the recruiting process and the games — and enjoying life.

My Aching Back

One of the few disputes we had with Todd was over his reluctance to ask for things that he needed. Many times he would just quietly do without, and we would become so frustrated. "Todd, just let us know what you need, and we'll be glad to get it for you," we'd say. He would seemingly make us guess what he needed.

I have suffered chronic pain for most of my adult life. On times when it got really bad, I would have to stay on the floor for days and, as I called it, live like a dog. Of course, Jane took very good care of me and Todd during those times.

But it was during one of those times that I understood a little of what Todd was feeling. I wanted just to do without rather than bother my wife so much. There's nothing like being in someone else's shoes to truly understand what they are feeling.

A Shocking Sight

In his teenage years, his doctor put rods in Todd's back to help with his severe scoliosis. He was having difficulty breathing normally and had to hold on to the handles of his chair to support himself enough to breathe. Even though the surgery straightened him up and made him look so grown up, it came with additional problems.

The first set of rods caused pressure sores to begin developing. Then some of the cable had to be removed. Then a set came loose and had to be replaced with a different kind that attached to his sacrum.

After that, we were constantly checking to make sure his back was not breaking down. One night when I rolled him over, we saw a shocking sight. It looked as if the rods were coming through the skin on his back.

Panicking, we called the doctor in the middle of the night. "I think the rods have come loose and are protruding through his back," I told him. The doctor didn't believe me and said, "It would have had to pull all the way through the sacrum." The doctor told us to bring him the next morning.

When I was carefully getting him out of the car,

Todd said, "Dad, please don't drop me." I told him, "Don't worry, your dad is not going to drop you." (If I was able to give that kind of assurance, just think how much more our Heavenly Father can take care of us.)

I'll never forget the look on the doctor's face when he first examined Todd. For a moment, even he seemed shocked, and I don't think he was sure as what to do. But he eventually gathered his composure and was able to come up with a plan. (I think we all expect doctors to be cheerful, and we tend to judge them when they are not. But we forget what they might have just experienced with a previous patient. This doctor had to go into the next room and try to put this out of his mind. Doctors are humans first, and they deserve our love and prayers.)

The rods indeed had pulled through Todd's sacrum and had to be removed because of infection. He had to spend the next six months lying down, mostly in a special reclining wheelchair, to allow healing. Eventually his spine fused back, and, thankfully, his back was much straighter than before.

Happy Kayaking

We were fortunate to meet so many special people and have them be a part of our lives. One of them was our second orthopedic doctor, whom I'll call Doctor Fred. His desire was that special-needs kids would be able to enjoy life to the fullest. One could tell they were more than just patients to him — they were people first. He took over after our first orthopedic doctor passed away, and he had the same genuine love for his patients.

He headed a local organization known as Limitless Sports. One of the activities was wheelchair basketball. Another activity he started was adaptive water skiing. (Water skiing? Are you sure?) The kids had so much fun! It was made possible first by so many doctors, nurses and other volunteers who were willing to give of their time to help. Second, it was made possible by special skis — essentially a seat and a ski on each side for balance. What fun the kids had with this each year! Todd was not a daredevil and didn't want to do the skiing, but he did want to attend and be part of the group.

One year an organization from Columbia came with kayaks and canoes. Todd looked on with interest but was fearful about trying it. The next year, a very nice man came up to Todd and told him how much fun it would be to get out on the water. Todd was not sure, but the man would not take no for an answer. The man said, "I'm coming back in just a little bit and get you out there."

It took only about five seconds for Todd to fall in love with kayaks. It was literally life-changing for him. He would have stayed out all day except for the hot South Carolina sun. I'm sure the man had no idea how happy he had made Todd just by caring and taking a little time with someone he didn't even know. For years afterward, Todd couldn't wait to get to the lake and into a kayak.

A Difficult Chair

Todd was growing up and had outgrown his fifth wheelchair. We were fortunate that he was able to use his upper body to help in transferring himself to and from his chair. But each chair is a little different. We had come up with different techniques to safely transfer him without hurting Todd — or our backs. However, this particular chair presented some different challenges. Even though it fit him well and he looked comfortable in it, I could not figure out how to transfer him into it.

I prayed, "God, please give me the wisdom to solve this problem." I didn't mention it to Todd, as I did not want him to worry. He was always considerate, as he knew I had a bad back. However, I believe it was the very next time I was helping him that, almost magically, Todd lifted himself into the air and landed softly in his chair.

I know that my mouth came open. "Todd, how did you do that?" He had simply grabbed the new arm support and, with me steadying him, picked himself up. Prayers aren't always answered that quickly, but I was so thankful for that one!

A Wing and a Prayer

It was completely terrifying. We were on our annual Labor Day weekend trip to Myrtle Beach. (We had begun doing this many years before as a type of family therapy after the loss of my mom to cancer. How much she would have loved to be with us!) Now, in the middle of the night, a severe storm knocked out power to our condominium and flooded the streets.

We were all in bed when Todd suddenly started screaming that he was dying and could not get his breath. It was a living nightmare. All he could say was that he was about to die. We were at a loss as to what to do. Here we were, on the tenth floor, with no elevator and the streets flooded, and our son in a desperate condition. And we had no idea why.

After a while, the power came on, and we were able to take Todd to the hospital in Myrtle Beach. He evidently did not have a lot of confidence in Jane and me, as he wanted his Aunt Donna to go with us. Donna was a registered nurse. (My sister Kay had also become a nurse, but he wanted his Aunt Donna — maybe because she was older.) At the hospital, they were not able to determine what was wrong, and Todd seemed to be getting better.

Later in the day, his symptoms returned. We

were determined not to go through another night like the one before, so we decided to make the three-hour trip to Todd's doctors in Columbia. Again, he was gasping for breath and saying he was about to die. I wasn't sure how I could make the drive with our son so sick, so I tried to separate my mind from what was going on in the rear of the van as Jane took care of him and tried to comfort him.

Todd once again didn't seem to have much confidence in his parents. He finally said, "This morning I had Aunt Donna with me, but now all I have is a wing and a prayer!" The doctors were never able to determine what went wrong other than possibly a reaction to medicine. But the experience made us even more thankful for the good times, and for life itself.

Family and Friends

We were so fortunate to have Todd in our family, and if you had asked him, he would have told you how fortunate he was to have his family. Both sides of our family loved him unconditionally. There was not one person he did not have special feelings for. His cousins and aunts and uncles and grandparents were all so special, and he savored being around them and simply experiencing life with them.

Some family members lived out of state, and he always looked forward to seeing his aunts and uncles and cousins from Virginia and California or talking with them on the phone. No one in our family looked on him as an incomplete person, but instead respected and loved him for who he was.

All of Todd's grandparents were special. Jane's dad and my mom never got to see him grow up, but they loved him beyond words while they were alive.

It was always special to travel the few miles to visit my dad. When friends added a ramp to his house for us, it made visiting so much easier. Sundays were very special, as my entire family would meet there after church for lunch. Bert (my brother) and Darrell (my brother-in-law) would always address Todd by the name of a not-too-popular president — just kidding him, of course. Todd loved it. Our family is still privileged to eat together at my dad's house (which is where my brother Kevin lives) almost every Sunday. It's like having Thanksgiving every week (and, in fact, it is something to be thankful for).

Jane's mom, Evelyn Rutland, dedicated her last years to helping take care of Todd. What a special relationship they developed! After his birth, while we were both working, she took care of him. We had just built a new house a few months before Todd was born, and had it not been for Jane's mom, we probably would have lost our home.

When Todd was older, she attended a private school, Orangeburg Prep, with him through seventh grade in order to assist him. It was just amazing to us how nice everyone was. Any accommodation that we needed was provided with a joyful spirit — no special meetings or red tape. We felt we were treated like royalty.

Later, Jane quit teaching and stayed home to home-school Todd until he graduated. Jane's mom also continued to help take care of Todd, even though there were days when she did not feel like it.

Unplanned

It was Sanctity of Life Sunday, a day designated by Southern Baptists to celebrate the value of life. I was to teach Sunday school that morning on this subject.

While I was getting ready, Jane came in and showed me the results of a positive pregnancy test. I had often heard of morning sickness, and instantly I knew what it meant, as I almost threw up.

But in just a few minutes, I became excited. We were going to be parents again! We had often thought of having another child but had resisted — partly because of the stress of taking care of Todd, and partly because of the fear of having another child with disabilities. Would we have the energy and resources take care of another?

As the days went by, we could hardly contain ourselves. We finally told our family, and the excitement was contagious. We began cleaning out the spare bedroom and making plans and picking out names — all of the things that expectant parents do, almost as if it were our first. But in just a few weeks, Jane began having problems, and we lost the child.

The pain and loss was almost unbearable.

By then, we had decided that, yes, we did want another child. However, we lost two more, and each time it was a very painful experience. We were never able to have another child.

But it was during these times that I realized, even more, how wrong abortion was. I had always been opposed to abortion, but now I was even more convinced.

I believe that life begins at conception, and, if you want to argue, very shortly after, as the heart begins beating in about twenty-two days. During our last pregnancy, we listened to the beautiful sound of the heartbeat and watched it on the ultrasound. A couple of weeks later, the doctor told us our child was no longer alive, as there was no heartbeat.

When there is a heartbeat, there is life. If these children were not alive, then how could their deaths have caused so much pain and sorrow? God is the one who gives life and takes it. We should not try to be God.

The problem with pro-choice is that the one who

has the most to lose does not have a choice.

I recently saw a former abortion doctor on television. He had performed 1,200 abortions prior to his life-changing moment. He and his wife lost their six-year-old child in an accident. She died in her parents' arms on the way to the hospital. He came to the realization that life was real and valued. Even though he had deep regrets about the children he had aborted, he became involved in the pro-life movement.

When we look around and see life being considered as cheap, should we be surprised? Our nation has put a low value on life, and it permeates our society. We had a pastor once who said, "God will not continue to allow a nation to exist that does not value the unborn."

However, the good news is God offers forgiveness and healing through Jesus Christ to those who have made the wrong choice. And before we look down our noses at others who have sinned, we should look at our own lives. In fact, the Bible says we are all sinners and in need of forgiveness. "For all have sinned and fall short of the glory of God" (Romans 3:23). Our only hope is in Jesus: "If you confess with your mouth Jesus as Lord, and believe in your heart that God raised Him from the dead, you will be saved" (Romans 10:9-11).

True Love Shows

Todd was getting older, and it was becoming more and more difficult to lift him out of his chair and into the backseat of our car.

My brother Bert organized a raffle to help raise money to purchase a specialized minivan that was remanufactured to accommodate wheelchairs. The local volunteer fire department also did some fundraisers. With both of these efforts, and with the help of a lot of friends and family, we were able to purchase a like-new van that tremendously enriched Todd's life. We were able to go places and do things that would have been almost impossible otherwise. It would be difficult to put into words our thanks to the many people who contributed, in addition to the ones who organized the fundraisers.

We are fortunate to be part of a very caring

church. Whatever we needed for Todd to attend church was provided — from moving his class to the ground level, to installing a hallway lift so that he would not have to be in the weather when going to the fellowship hall, to paving a spot where we parked. Even a special parking spot was paved at our ball field so he could watch the games on a level area. We never had to beg; in fact, we never had to even ask. Whatever he needed was provided. True love is expressed more by actions than by words.

Dixie's Accident

"Daddy, watch out for Dixie!" Todd was always cautioning us when we pulled out of our drive. I told him, "It's almost impossible to run over that big dog with this low van while we're going so slow."

Dixie was Todd's golden retriever and loving companion. Dixie had been a gift from Todd's cousin and her husband, Kayla and Richard. We had searched the internet for the perfect companion dog, and goldens seemed to fit what we were wanting. Todd was grown by then, and we thought a golden would be a good companion for him.

If they don't destroy your home during the chewing stage as puppies, they are the most loving of dogs. Dixie loved Todd so much. Many times she would go back to Todd's bed and lick him profusely, just as if Todd was her child. And, of course, Todd loved her. Whenever we would walk on our street, Dixie would lie down at the edge of our yard and cry, wanting to go with us. We could hear her almost the entire walk.

Our minivan had a lowered floor, which allowed for easier accessibility. However, the downside was that even speed bumps would scrape the bottom of the van. We had an underground fence to prevent Dixie from going into the road when she was outside. But she was still vulnerable to our vehicle.

I thought I was always being careful, but I found out how fast accidents can happen. Todd and I were going to the church one evening to watch our church's softball team play. (It was one of Todd's favorite things to do. There are so many good memories of spending warm evenings watching various church teams play. My brother Kevin still holds the batting average there. Every time he batted, he hit an inside-the-park home run! Of course, it was helpful that the opposing team had quite a few "errors" while he was running the bases. The other church members were always patient in allowing him to bat. After he had batted his one time, he would put his bat back in the bag and eat one of the world's finest Two Mile Swamp hot dogs.)

I had just started to move slowly from our parking place when it felt like the van had run over a speed bump. It was then that I saw a sickening sight: Dixie limping off to one side. Shocked, I told Todd, "I just ran over Dixie!" To this day, I don't know how it happened. However, I knew it was probably a devastating injury, as the tire had seemingly run over her body. That night I fought back tears, fearing she had suffered internal injuries. I prayed that God would spare Todd's buddy. Dixie went back to Todd's room to sleep that night, something she had never done before.

Miraculously, she did not suffer a serious injury that required her to go to the vet. Later, Todd told me, "Dad, I would have forgiven you if Dixie had died. I know it was just an accident." I felt so guilty for allowing the accident to happen, but it made me feel so good to have such a forgiving son.

Love's Invention

From almost the time Todd could talk, he loved to sing. (Before he could talk, he "directed" music by moving his hands up and down.) We could usually tell if he was feeling well by his singing. He sang constantly and developed a beautiful deep voice. His favorite songs were from his favorite season, Christmas. He would sing Christmas songs year round.

As he grew older and wanted to sing in the choir, I'd carry him up the steps to the choir loft and then place his wheelchair there. Later, my brother Bert would help carry him in his chair up the steps. After some years, it became quite a task, and we'd recruit help from church members.

As part of moving the chair up the steps, I'd move the "tippy" bars around so they would not catch on the steps and cause an accident. The bars were supposed to prevent the chair from tipping over backwards. However, one time when we came down, I forgot to turn them back. As soon as Todd started moving, the chair flipped over, scaring both of us to death, but thankfully causing no injury.

Bruce was one of our friends, and he came up with what he thought was a solution to our "growing" choir problem. At his place of work, they used a small electric lift that he thought could be adapted to our choir loft. Our church agreed to allow him to install it. He tore out the steps and installed his custom version of the lift. Then he placed an addition to the choir floor so that Todd's chair would have room to turn safely. It worked perfectly and was such a tremendous help.

Todd had not been able to even practice because of the tremendous effort to get into the choir. Now he was able to practice and sing anytime with just the push of a button. Isn't it amazing what just a little love and compassion can accomplish? Yes, even the impossible can be made possible!

Our Favorite Place

Our family always looked forward to trips to the beach. The gentle waves and fresh breeze under the warm South Carolina sun made problems seem a world away.

One year we bought a raft so that Todd could sit on it and be more comfortable at the edge of the water. Sometimes when the tide is moving, the ocean will leave pools near the edge of the water where there are shelves in the sand. Todd used his hands, much like moving a wheelchair, to move the raft in the pools. What a delight it was for him! I think it gave him a sense of freedom to move on his own. As he grew older, he enjoyed using a "reacher" tool to pluck shells from the sand.

However, time brought two problems: he had gained weight, and we had gotten older. There is one thing that wheelchairs don't work well with, and that is soft sand. But when you know your child loves something so much, you don't give up on it very easily. How could we continue to get him out to one of God's most enjoyable creations?

One year, I carried boards and tried to "leap frog" them out to the hard sand. Moving the boards proved almost as hard as dragging the chair through the sand. We tried different versions of that arrangement, and none worked very well. The sand seemed to be winning. Jane came up with the idea of using simple straw beach mats, the kind that people use to sun themselves. I didn't think it was a very good idea, but we tried it, and to my surprise it worked better than anything else I had tried.

It was during these times that we met some of the nicest and most considerate people. Most times during our efforts, volunteers would just come up and ask if they could help us. Of course we never turned them down. And when we did have to ask for help, we were never turned down. I doubt that those who helped really knew how happy they had just made Todd. Little things in life, especially for ones with disabilities, can have such a huge impact.

I'm not sure how we learned about wheelchair beach mats; maybe it was through my searching the Internet in an attempt to find a solution. However, many beaches were installing rubber "sidewalks" on beaches to allow accessibility. They were expensive but life-changing for those with disabilities who might otherwise never enjoy the beach. The beach we visited did not have them. They did have ramps, but the ramps ended up in deep sand. Such ramps might as well have been a set of stairs, as they were almost useless for those in wheelchairs.

This beach did offer special wheelchairs designed for the sand. However, they didn't fit a lot of people that needed extra support. And there was also the problem of transferring someone out of one chair and into another. That process is not really simple when you're unable to stand and your parents aren't very strong.

We began writing to different news organizations, trying to bring the problem to the public's attention. None responded to us. Finally, our state representative suggested we contact a particular person with the North Myrtle Beach Chamber of Commerce. It turned out he was very understanding and considerate. They agreed to look into the matter and did install the first mat in 2011 as a test. Although it did not go out as far as we had hoped, it was a start and did allow access to the beach for some who did not have the ability to otherwise get there. The next year they told me they had good results with the first mat and would probably expand use to areas where ramps were not an option. I'm hopeful that others will notice and continue to encourage this beach and other beaches to use these mats.

Another business that we encountered at North Myrtle Beach was the Lost Treasure Golf miniature golf course. We had noticed the sign about it being wheelchair accessible. How rare it was to find places actually catering to the disabled. To our delight, it was completely accessible, from the train that carried players to the top of the course, to each hole being designed to accommodate wheelchairs. At one place, there was even a drawbridge that would be lowered to allow wheelchairs to cross the railroad track. We had so much fun there for many years, and it probably did not cost any more to construct than a normal course.

People with disabilities have so many problems, and little can be done about some of those problems. However, problems of accessibility should be corrected when at all possible. Just a few inches in a doorway can be the same as six feet to someone in a wheelchair.

We have suggested that business owners consider renting a wheelchair for a day and using it around their place of business. It would probably be eye-opening. We've seen places with really nice handicapped parking, but with doors that would take a small gorilla to open! Recently, I used a handicapped-accessible restroom and almost could not get the door open to let myself out!

We urge businesses, churches and other public places to evaluate their facilities from the disability side of things. Not because of any law, but out of compassion. Compassion and love will make much more of a difference than any law ever could. We feel the city of North Myrtle Beach and the Lost Treasure Golf Course began acting out of compassion, and we hope they will continue to do so.

Please Don't Do That

Unless one has dealt with disabilities, sometimes it is easy to take for granted facilities designed to help. I admit I never gave much thought to special measures to help the handicapped before our son was born.

One of my pet peeves is people who park in handicapped parking places and are not handicapped or those who leave shopping carts in those spaces. For us, it was merely an aggravation to have to move carts in order to park; but for some, it means not being able to park, or worse, maybe not even being able to get back into their vehicle because they don't have the ability to move the carts out of the way.

One day I was moving carts from a parking place so that I could park our van. I turned around, and a man was placing another cart where I had just moved one. Irritated, I bluntly told him that those spaces were not for carts but for handicapped parking. He apologized and moved the cart. I could tell that he really meant no harm. He was just like I might have been at one time, ignorant of the potential problem he might be causing.

I turned around the other way, and another man was leaving a cart behind me. Now I was really mad, and I told him in no uncertain terms that those spaces were not for carts. However, this man was not as accommodating and began arguing as he made his way back to his vehicle.

Neither man had seen Todd waiting inside the van for me to park. We had permanent handicapped plates on the rear of the van rather than a temporary sign that hung from the mirror. As this second man began pulling away, the rear window rolled down, and a very angry woman stuck her head out and wanted to know where my handicapped plate was. At this, I really lost my temper, opened the van, grabbed Todd's chair and jerked it down the ramp. Pointing at him, I said, "There's my handicapped plate!"

The conversation was over, and even though I didn't set a very good example for Todd or my wife, hopefully it made an impression on others to respect handicapped-marked parking spots and to be considerate of the less fortunate.

Dixie and Santa

Thankfully, the parking lot story was the exception in our lives. Our family received so many gifts and acts of kindness from family, friends and even strangers, it's impossible to remember them all. The world can be a very cruel place, but it also has many very kind people who, by their actions, give value to life itself.

One gift was from Santa Claus. When we picked up our dog Dixie, the breeder told us, "Don't expect this one to be a watchdog. She will probably help the crooks take items to their car." Goldens are probably the perfect family dog, so even-tempered and lovable.

However, Dixie would go crazy if you were wearing gloves, so any burglars would do well to leave their hands bare. Once, during a rare South Carolina snowfall, we all put on gloves to go outside and play in the snow. We had a difficult time enjoying the snow and staying warm while at the same time, a crazed dog was trying to remove our gloves!

One night during the Christmas season, while we were out, Santa Claus and his helpers broke into our house and installed a new large-screen, high-definition television so Todd could better enjoy the upcoming bowl games. Of course, Dixie just welcomed them into our house. Thankfully, these "crooks" were delivering, not taking — and not wearing gloves!

Politician Grown Up

I have already mentioned Todd's early interest in politics. Now that he was a young adult, it had evolved to this: "Dear Kenneth," the letter would begin. Then the congressman or senator would continue on, talking about his position on a certain matter. I wondered why I was getting a letter from a congressman. I had not written anything to him. Then, inevitably, Todd would say, "Dad, I emailed him about that."

Todd cared very deeply about America and about many moral and social issues. He learned that the power of the pen still existed, and we encouraged him to be involved. (All it takes is just a little time, especially in the Internet age. A pen is not even needed! What would be accomplished if more people took this attitude, including myself, and stood up for what was right?)

Finally, I told him one day, "Todd, you need to sign your name, not mine." I kidded with him: "I don't want to open the door one day and have my kneecaps broken!"

Ministries We Love

Many of the things our family became involved in were because of our experiences with Todd. Many of these experiences forever changed our lives. Following are some of the ministries we came to appreciate.

Joni and Friends

It was back in the 1970s, and I remember volunteering to help with a movie that was going to be shown at a local theater. It was produced by Worldwide Pictures, a division of Billy Graham Ministries. Worldwide Pictures used local volunteers to assist with their ministries. The movie was shown by renting the theater, and then the money was collected and sent to Worldwide Pictures. The theater collected the concessions for themselves, which I guess was an extra incentive for the theater to show the movie.

This particular movie was about a young lady

named Joni Eareckson, who had suffered a devastating neck injury when she dove into shallow water. I don't remember if I had already read her book or not at the time. But I had no idea how much Joni's ministry, which is known as JAF Ministries now, was going to be a part of my life in later years.

There are millions of disabled people worldwide, and most of them do not have access to the medical equipment they need to assist them. But despite their disabilities, each one is loved by God. Their disabilities and lack of resources make them no less a person.

I read about a man who went on a trip to Guatemala. He saw a man who was unable to walk crawling through the mud. He also saw a woman pushing her husband in a wheelbarrow. He promised that he would return with wheelchairs, and a ministry was born. That ministry, now part of JAF Ministries, is known as Wheels for the World. I donated one of Todd's first wheelchairs to that ministry after I read about the impact they were making.

One day we were at Todd's wheelchair provider's

office, selecting a new chair. I just happened to mention to him that I'd be giving Todd's old chair to a ministry that sends chairs to Third World countries. He said, "Really? Do you want some more? I've got a whole room full, and there's nothing I can do with them."

It was that conversation that led me to investigate and find that there was such a tremendous need. All I had to do was collect the chairs and coordinate getting them to one of the regional collectors. Wow! What a joy that has been! I've picked them up from garbage dumps and even bought one, with a friend's help, from a pawn shop. Each chair is life-changing, possibly for eternity. Chairs are carried to regional prisons where they are completely renovated. There, prisoners do the work, and many of them have been able to accomplish something for good for the first time in their lives. The chairs are then shipped to other countries, where teams of medical personnel custom-fit the chairs to the appropriate recipient. Of course, the gospel is also presented, and many entire families have come to know Christ.

There was a story that I saw on the JAF website about a little girl name Amee, who was born in Thailand. She, like Todd, was born with spina bifida. Because the stigma of the disability was so great, her mother had abandoned her. Her dad could not bring himself to discard her in the jungle, so he took care of Amee as best as he could. But this meant leaving her by the road all day long as he tried to make a living farming.

One of the ministry associates of Joni and Friends rescued her from the dirt and lifted her into a pink wheelchair. Amee could not stop giggling with joy. She was able to go to an orphanage, where her father could visit. It was determined that the men at the Arizona state prison were the ones who had restored her chair. Seeing the photo of Amee touched their lives, too! She has since been adopted by a loving Christian family.

In the Bible, we see in 2 Samuel 9 how King David showed compassion on one of King Saul's grandsons, Mephibosheth, son of Johnathan. Mephibosheth was lame in both feet. King David treated him as one of his sons and commanded that land be given back to him and that the produce of the land be given to him for his support. Despite Mephibosheth's disability, King David valued him.

Todd's Missionary Friends

How lovely on the mountains are the feet of him who brings good news, who announces peace and brings good news of happiness, who announces salvation and says to Zion, "Your God reigns!" (Isaiah 52:7)

Almost twenty years ago, a local pastor (I'll call him Albert) befriended Todd. They had a lot in common, and Albert was even a Gamecock! Later, as the years passed, Todd had a knack for keeping up with Albert when he moved on to different ministries. Eventually, he even located Albert by email when he became a foreign missionary.

After all of those years, Todd learned that he was back in the States and asked him, by email, if he was interested in supplying at our church while we were without a pastor. To our delight, he said he would be happy to discuss this with our church during his transition back to being a pastor. During this time, Todd and Albert were able to rekindle their friendship.

On one Sunday, Albert preached a sermon about the importance of lifting up our missionaries with our moral support. His sermon was something to the effect that we tend to fire off and then forget missionaries, much like a ship launching a missile. In other words, we send missionaries out and then forget about them.

Albert knew this firsthand, since he had been a missionary for several years. He was not bitter, but he was trying to educate Christians about a much-needed ministry. This was right up Todd's alley. He loved reaching out to missionaries who had come to our church. He would usually collect email addresses so that he could keep in touch.

In this case, we had never met these missionaries, but Albert connected Todd with a foreign missionary he knew personally and had served with. Todd loved writing to him and was planning on sending the first care package to him when he got sick. What a joy it was reaching out to this family, many thousands of miles away, and bringing a little joy to someone who had sacrificed so much.

Compassion Child

"For I was hungry and you gave me something to eat, I was thirsty and you gave me something to drink, I was a stranger and you invited me in, I needed clothes and you clothed me, I was sick and you looked after me, I was in prison and you came to visit me. Then the righteous will answer him, 'Lord, when did we see you hungry and feed you, or thirsty and give you something to drink? When did we see you a stranger and invite you in, or needing clothes and clothe you? When did we see you sick or in prison and go to visit you?' The King will reply, 'Truly I tell you, whatever you did for one of the least of these brothers and sisters of mine, you did for me.'" (Matthew 25:35-40)

One of our favorite things do to as a family was to attend Christian concerts. We all loved Christian music and the many different groups.

One concert we attended was life-changing. I believe it was Casting Crowns in concert at the Colonial Center in Columbia. We really liked this group, and you could just tell they had a heart for Jesus.

During the concert, they promoted an organization known as Compassion International, whose purpose was to encourage families to "adopt" a child and to support him or her financially each month. As an alternative, we could just give some money as a one-time gift during an offering time.

When the offering bucket was passed to us, I asked my wife to put in a few dollars. I've told friends since then that it was really a "guilt offering." It was an offering not given from the heart. "Okay, we've given something, and now I can just wash my hands of this need," I thought.

However, the next time they were talking about these kids, God began speaking to me very clearly. I thought, "I really can't afford to pay the thirty-five dollars a month." But then it was as if God asked me, "What if this was your child? Could you afford it then?" I had to admit that I could. Then again, it was as if God told me to go and pick out a child, as He had one for us.

After the concert, I asked Jane if she would like to support a child. To my surprise, there was no hesitation, and said she would. We decided on a precious little girl from Brazil (whom we will just call Beatriz). What a blessing it was to see her grow over the years and to receive letters from her about her life. We sent her pictures of our family and have tried to encourage her.

Many of these kids do not feel valued. Their families struggle to live. It is gratifying just to be able to support them financially and show that someone they don't even know loves them. Hopefully it may help them realize their life is valued.

We have since had the privilege of attending other concerts, only now as Compassion International volunteers, helping others have the joy and life-changing chance of adopting kids.

Our Walk Through the Valley

Nausea was something that Todd battled most of his life. He took medication for acid reflux, which helped dramatically, but, still, it was a part of life. So the fact that he had thrown up was not that alarming. But then it continued. His fever went up, and he just did not look well.

I usually tried to keep gas in the van, but this was a night when I had not done my job, and it was low. I had to go and find a station open in the middle of the night before we could carry Todd to the hospital.

Once we were there, the doctors determined that he had a urinary infection and a hernia that might be causing an obstruction. An NG tube was inserted to remove fluid from his stomach. It was a very uncomfortable procedure, but it helped him feel better. He soon improved, and the tests showed nothing else alarming. The doctor said they would fix the hernia in the future, after Todd got over the hospitalization.

It was almost Thanksgiving, and we were all thankful to be able to go home and enjoy the holidays. Todd always enjoyed that time of year. He would have put up the Christmas tree in October if we had let him.

That Wednesday night at church before Thanksgiving, as we discussed the prayer list, Todd said, "Take me off that list. I'm good." Everything seemed to be moving past our recent crisis.

On Sunday night, the extreme nausea started again, and his fever went back up. Jane and I debated as to whether to carry him back to the hospital. After a while, it seemed that was what we should do, as the nausea was getting worse. On the way, Todd started singing. He always sang when he felt good. I wondered if we had acted too quickly, but decided to continue and get him checked out.

There did not seem to be any cause for alarm. He was thought to still have an infection and was admitted to the hospital. The next day the nausea got severe, and another NG tube was inserted. Todd did not want that and begged for them to wait for me to get there from work, but, of course, they could not.

That night, a nurse a kept close check on him and commented that his heart rate was high. I was not particularly alarmed, as his heart rate had been high for years. But then, during the night, Todd started saying strange things. He told me that it must be the medicine. He was actually in respiratory arrest, and carbon dioxide was building up, affecting his thinking.

I also noticed strange sweat on his brow, almost like he had malaria. I would read, months later, in a book by Joni Eareckson Tada that sweating is actually a sign of pain in paraplegics. I had never heard this before.

The next thing I knew, the nurse picked up the phone and called for a rapid response to Todd's room. We could not believe it was happening. Doctors and nurses from all over the hospital converged on us and in just a little while Todd was in ICU.

He still did not seem to be very critical, and we went back and visited with him and talked with him.

Todd probably felt much worse than he let us know. He had always been very reluctant to tell us when he felt bad.

However, Todd soon went into complete respiratory arrest. I thought we were going to lose him that day. I called my family and told them that Todd was very bad. But then he was placed on a ventilator and almost immediately began getting better.

After a few days, he was able to get off the ventilator. He still was not himself though, mentally. A turning point came one evening while he was still in ICU, before I got there. One of his favorite songs came on the television, "Let It Snow." His mother said he mouthed every word behind the oxygen mask he was wearing. We were ecstatic! Our son was making his way back.

The doctor told us that this time he would fix the hernia before we left the hospital. But Todd could not get over his fever. There was debate between the doctors as to whether he had pneumonia in his lungs, as one said, or infection in his stomach, as another thought. This went on for a several weeks.

Todd was in good spirits and enjoyed visits from friends and family. A friend was gracious enough to let us borrow her computer tablet. Todd was finally able to connect back to the electronic world that he loved so much and catch up on Facebook. I made a small sort of desk out of cardboard to assist him in holding the tablet, since he was lying down.

The room was so small, there was barely enough room for the three of us to sleep. One night, I heard Todd call my name. Thinking something was wrong, I climbed over the cots and rushed over to his bedside. "What's wrong?" I asked. "What time is it?" he asked. After that, I found a clock that I could tie to his bed rails.

The doctor finally made the decision to do the hernia surgery. Todd just did not seem like he would get well until it was performed. The doctor told us the surgery would be a few hours unless something else showed up. We told him we thought he would find something else besides the hernia, as Todd had just been too sick.

After about six hours, we were becoming

alarmed. Something must be wrong. Why hadn't the electronic flasher gone off to signal we could go talk with the doctor? Finally, it did, and we were excited to be through with this part of his recovery.

However, the attendant at the desk told us to keep the mobile flasher; the doctor just needed to talk with us. As the doctor began telling us and our pastor what he had found, it was almost as if we were reliving the day Todd was born. There was so much he found wrong that it seemed like a bad dream.

Scar tissue had caused several places in his intestine to rupture, causing infection. He needed permission to do a colostomy. He would place Todd back in ICU after the surgery. Of course, we were willing for him to do whatever it took to get our son well.

On top of all of his other problems, Todd also contracted a "super bug" that was resistant to antibiotics. Everyone had to wear gloves and a gown when visiting.

A Very Kind Nurse

After several days in the ICU, Todd was beginning to

look pretty scruffy. Because of the ventilator, we could not shave him easily. A very kind older nurse was taking care of him one night. When we came back to see him, he was all cleaned up and looked like his old self again. We were so delighted, despite his serious condition, to have our son looking so good.

When we thanked the nurse, she simply told us, "There are some things beyond my control, but there are some things that I can do to help families, and this was one of them." Helping patients look better, and families feel better, was what she could do. It might have seemed to others like a small and not-so-unusual thing. But to a family in crisis, it was a special gift that we will never forget.

Her action was a testimony that should inspire us to use our gifts from God, however small they may seem. There are things that we can't do anything about, but that should not prevent us from doing the things we can. Small things — even things that we think don't even matter — can have such a tremendous impact on people.

Why Are You Crying, Daddy?

Jane called me at work. (I had been trying to work during the day and drive back at night to stay with them.) "Please hurry," she said. "Todd is not doing well and it has been a very bad day."

When I got there, he was saying things out of his head again. He was saying, "I'm in the wrong hospital." And he asked for a hamburger. He had not eaten for weeks, and always loved to eat. Then he would say, "I'm in the wrong hospital." The words still haunt me. Then, "Please, let me go outside." Then he would say, "I'm in the wrong hospital," almost chanting it. If you knew him, you knew he rarely complained and would never have wanted to worry or upset us.

Finally, after several hours, he looked at me and said, "Who are you?" It was at that point that Jane and I started crying. Our only child did not know his parents. All of the weeks of stress finally were coming out. Our emotions were shot.

A minute later, he looked up at me and said, "Why are you crying, Daddy?" It was maybe the last thing he said to us.

One of my favorite verses in the Bible is Revelation 7:17: "For the Lamb in the center of the throne shall be their shepherd and shall guide them to springs of the water of life: and God shall wipe every tear from their eyes." I wondered if God sent us a reminder through our son.

It was not many more days before Todd went to be with Jesus. It was New Year's Day. As we all stood around his bed, a nurse said, "I can see the love in this room for him. I can't say that about everyone."

Since then, we have shed buckets of tears, and I understand that is normal. The only thing that has gotten us through is the promise of the future for those who are in Christ. We know that Todd is there, not because of who he was, but because of his faith in Jesus and who Jesus was. One day there will be no more tears, or pain, or death.

Wheelchairs would probably roll really well on golden streets, much better than they do crossing the deep sand dunes of Myrtle Beach. However, they would be useless and will not exist in heaven.

Todd died on January 1, 2013. The Gamecocks

were playing Michigan that day in a very big Capital One Bowl game. It was the same game in which Jadeveon Clowney delivered "The Hit," which is now famous. Some well-meaning friends suggested that Todd was watching and had enjoyed the Gamecocks' big victory. Later, I started thinking about that. Even if it was possible to watch a football game from heaven, I don't think we would. We forget to consider the majesty that will be before us. Would we watch a game, or would we prefer to worship the King of Kings and Lord of Lords? It would not even be a choice!

A friend who was a student nurse and attended Todd's birth as part of her training posted the following on Todd's Facebook page:

> *Years ago, as a young student nurse, I was excited to attend my first ever birth of a baby. A couple from my own hometown were expecting a baby with complications. I was honored to attend this birth, but saddened to know there were additional complications that*

came as a surprise once the baby was delivered. I knew, though, that this baby had wonderful God-fearing parents that were loved by a community of close-knit, supportive family and friends. No matter the handicaps of this child, he would be loved and cared for. So I was not surprised, when visiting my grandparents' church at Two Mile that Todd Sanford always rolled into church in his wheelchair with a smile on his face, and his Bible in his lap. Yes, there was a reason that God made him that way. He was meant to touch many lives, including mine. For a little boy who could never feel the ocean sand between his toes, I would now like to ask: How does it feel to walk on the streets of Gold? I will always remember you, one of my sweet babies. Much love and comfort to his parents, Kenny and Jane.

During the months following Todd's death, the grief and despair were at times almost more than we could bear. I wondered where God was during our time of trouble. When I heard Christian songs that had once inspired me, they no longer did. It was many months later when I was reminded how men so much closer to God than I, even the Apostle Paul, had suffered terribly while serving God. Paul wrote the following in 2 Corinthians 11: 24-27:

Five times I received from the Jews thirty-nine lashes. Three times I was beaten with rods, once I was stoned, three times I was shipwrecked, a night and a day I have spent in the deep. I have been on frequent journeys, in dangers from rivers, dangers from robbers, dangers from my countrymen, dangers from the Gentiles, dangers from the city, dangers in the wilderness, dangers on the sea, dangers from false brethren: I have been in labor and hardship, through many sleepless nights, in hunger and thirst, often without food, in cold and exposure.

All of this is spoken by one whom most call the greatest missionary to ever live. He was a man who was completely sold out to Jesus, whom he had met on the Damascus Road, despite his circumstances.

How arrogant I had been! I was driven to ask for forgiveness. My God did love us. He had not forgotten us! Even though there are times in this world when we may wonder and do not understand, He settled the question of love 2,000 years ago. All one has to do is look at the cross! Then you'll see: Amazing love, amazing grace!

Even though we cannot comprehend events in this world, we can depend on the truth that God has everything in control. In Job 38:4, we find these words: "Where were you when I laid the foundation of the earth? Tell Me, if you have understanding."

I waited patiently for the Lord; And He inclined to me, and heard my cry. He brought me up out of the pit of destruction, out of the miry clay; And He set my feet upon a rock making my footsteps firm. And He put a new song in my mouth, a song of praise to our God: Many will see and fear, And will trust in the Lord. (Psalms 40:1-3)

I mentioned earlier that our family had become Compassion International sponsors. When Todd passed, I really did not know how to tell our little "adopted" girl in Brazil. And I guess I just did not want to bring it up, so we did not write for a very long time. I finally received a letter, and I could tell she was wondering why she had not heard from us for such a long time. For many of these kids, just hearing and knowing that someone loves them means so much. We had failed to do this, and we finally had the composure to write the following letter:

Dear Beatriz,

For God so loved the world that He gave His only Begotten Son, that whosoever believes in Him shall not perish, but have everlasting life. (John 3:16)

We're so sorry that it has been so long

since we wrote to you. It has not been because we do not love you, it just has been a very difficult year for us. Our son Todd passed away in January after a short illness. We know, because of his faith in Jesus, we will see him again. It is that fact that gets us through and gives us hope for tomorrow. Our hope is that you, too, will come to know Jesus as your Savior, if you have not already trusted Him.

Thank you again for the beautiful drawings that you send to us. We look forward to getting them and hearing from you. We hope your family is well and that you are doing well in school. Take care for now.

Love, Kenny and Jane Sanford

Our hope and prayer is that we will one day meet Beatriz in heaven.

Todd's Missionary House

In the summer of 2012, only a short time before we lost Todd, some members from our church, including my sister-in-law Donna, went on a mission trip with two local partnering churches to the Dominican Republic. They were able to see firsthand the extreme poverty there. They also experienced how loving and appreciative the Dominican people were.

For the next trip in 2013, partnering with another church, it was decided that money would be raised to build a house for someone in the Dominican. Houses can be constructed there for as little as $5,000.

After the money was raised for the first house, funds were also donated, anonymously, for a house to be built in memory of Todd. That house was given to a man named Freddy and his family. The process was coordinated by a local missionary whom members got to know, Tony Salgado. Tony is from America, but felt called to full-time mission service in the Dominican Republic.

We were told that Freddy, the one who received Todd's house, had recently become a Christian. Freddy would go around in his community witnessing for Jesus.

On days that are dark for us, it helps us to know that Todd's house is providing a family some comfort where there was little before. Todd would have been so excited to see this.

Exactly a year to the day after Todd first became sick, I saw a post on Facebook from Tony Salgado. He mentioned that the government had given land for a church and that a man named Freddy had preached the gospel to everyone, even the mayor, as part of the ceremony. Could it be the same Freddy who had received Todd's house? I messaged Tony, and he soon replied that it was indeed the same Freddy. He added that the house had been such a blessing to Freddy's family.

Sometimes blessings come so unexpectedly. On the one-year anniversary of the day that our son had gotten sick, God reminded us that Todd's life was still blessing others and still being used by Him.

A Life's Impact

I have often heard people talk about having a broken heart. However, until you've experienced it, there is little chance that you can understand the amount of pain it involves.

I never knew such pain existed. But I also came to realize that the level of pain was related of the level of love that existed before the pain. It was better to have had that love and to endure the pain, than to never have had that love.

In Psalm 34:18, we find hope in God's care and love for us: "The Lord is near to the brokenhearted and saves those who are crushed in spirit."

Today, as I write this, years after Todd's death, it is still difficult for me to believe that our son is really gone. It still almost takes my breath away when I think about it.

Our loss can never be expressed in words, much

like Todd's gain in heaven. In 1 Corinthians 2:9, we read the promise: "Just as it is written, Things which eye has not seen and ear has not heard and which have not entered the heart of man, all that God has prepared for those who love Him."

We are also still overwhelmed by how blessed we were — not just to be parents, but parents of such a special young man.

Thousands of times during Todd's life, I thanked God for giving us our son. I still continue to thank Him today. But now my prayer is extended to thank God also for His Son, for it's because of His Son that we'll one day see our son again.

In John 11:25-26, Jesus said, "I am the resurrection and the life; he who believes in Me will live even if he dies, and everyone who lives and believes in Me will never die." Do you believe this? I'm thankful that this promise also included my son and any other person who believes in Jesus as Savior.

The two very special guys I've written about, and our unborn children, did impact their world. It is a testimony that all life matters. In His infinite wisdom, God can use broken bodies as a way to touch many people's lives and to heal broken spirits. He continues to use their lives today.

If you would like to contact us, please do so by email at whyareyoucryingdaddy@gmail.com. Thank you so much for taking the time to read these memories. Just writing these thoughts has provided much healing.

May our country turn back to God and once again begin to value life!

All honor and glory go to our Lord and Savior Jesus Christ — because He lives!